T0143681

F is for Florida

written by kids for kids

WESTWINDS
PRESS®

A is for **Art Deco**

Miami's art deco style is cool.
The buildings look like colorful jewels.

B

is for Beach

In Florida we invented sunscreen
for all those bodies muscled and lean.

C

is for Capital

Tallahassee should get a visit from you—
home of FAMU and FSU, too.

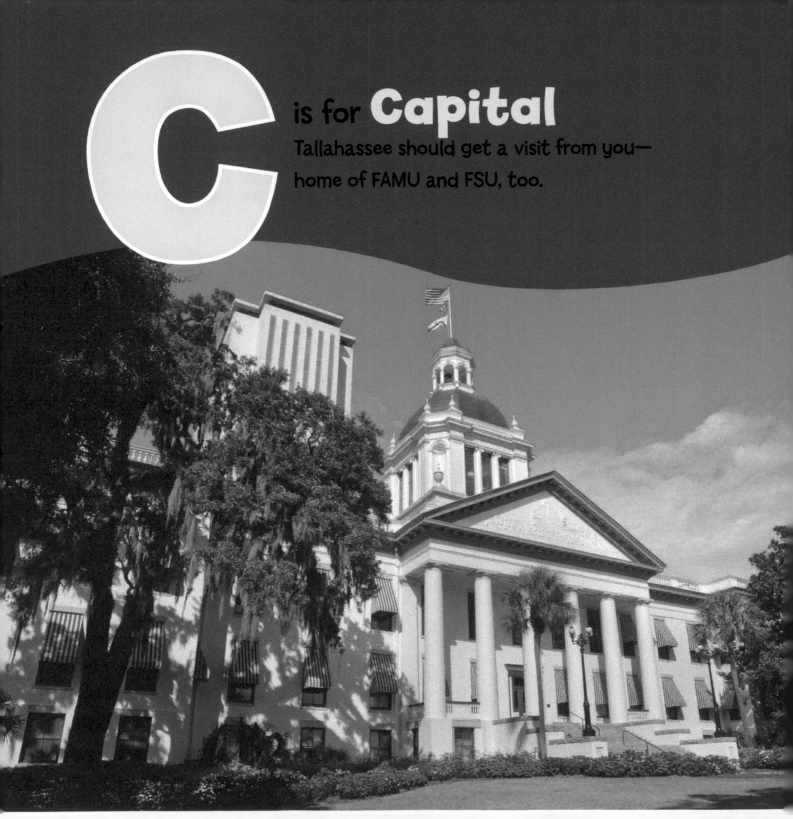

D is for

Daytona 500

Cars flying by, oh so fast,
cheer your favorite as it drives past.

E

is for **Everglades**

By boat, kayak, or canoe,

exploring these waters is fun to do.

F is for Fort

More than a hundred forts show our rich past.
What historic shadows they do cast.

G is for Gator

These reptiles have smiles big and wide.

Don't get too close . . . you don't want to be inside!

H is for **Hurricane**

The nation's biggest storms hit our shores.

With the wind and rain, you're better off indoors.

I

is for
Indigenous People

Our state had many
indigenous tribes;
now the Miccosukee and
Seminole people still thrive.

J

is for **Jacksonville**

Sitting in the northeast, so bright and pretty,
this is Florida's largest city.

90 Miles to CUBA

SOUTHERNMOST POINT

CONTINENTAL U.S.A.

KEY WEST, FL.
Home of the Sunset

K is for Key West

Seven Mile Bridge leads to the "Island of Bones,"
where the "conchs" will make you feel right at home.

L is for Lake Okeechobee

"The Lake" is what we call it, in case you didn't know, but some folks also call it the "Big O."

M is for **Manatee**

If you see one you will say, "Wow!"

Some call them "mermaids" or even "sea cows."

N

is for
Nesting Turtle

Hatchlings are born up on the beach,
then down to the ocean they must reach.

is for

Orange

We can buy them or
pick them right off the tree,
so juicy and good,
full of vitamin C.

P

is for

Panther

Check out this sleek,
majestic mammal!
No wonder it's the
official State Animal.

Q

is for
Quinceañera

It's a party for a girl
who's turning fifteen,
her day to be treated
just like a queen.

R is for Rocket

On the Space Coast, blastoff's what they do,
circling the Earth with a bird's-eye view.

S is for
Sea Life

Manatees and turtles you just might see,
but a lot more lies within our deep blue sea.

T

is for **Theme Park**

With tons of rides sure to make you dizzy,
our twenty-five theme parks will keep you busy.

U is for Underwater Research Lab
(Aquarius Reef Base)

You can study marine life from under the sea.
This lab is amazing, you will agree.

V is for **Vacation**

Hot and sunny most of the year—
Two reasons why tourists visit and cheer.

W

is for

Weeki Wachee Springs

If you thought mermaids could never be true, visit the Gulf Coast, you might see a few!

X

is for

eXtreme Sports

Flying over waves on a
board or jet ski,
there are thrills to be
had out on the sea.

y

is for **Yummy**

Key lime pie is a dessert most yummy,
Conch fritters also taste good in your tummy.

Z

is for **Zebra Longwing**

A caterpillar with big black spikes
becomes a butterfly with zebra stripes.

Who Knew?

Art Deco
This art style was popular in the 1920s and '30s, influencing everything from paintings to cars to fashion to architecture. Miami's art deco district has the largest concentration of art deco architecture in the world! With so many candy-colored hotels and apartments to see, it's best to take a walking tour.

Beach
No matter where you are in Florida, you're never more than 60 miles away from a beach. The state has an astonishing 1,350 miles of beaches. Miami Beach pharmacist Benjamin Green invented one of the first sunscreens in 1944. Called "Red Vet Pet," it was a red, sticky goo, like petroleum jelly, made for WWII soldiers to use in the tropics.

Capital
Tallahassee ("Tally" for short) became the state capital in 1824 because it was between West Florida and East Florida, two former Spanish colonies. It has the third-tallest capitol building in America—twenty-two stories! Tally is a college town—FSU is the city's oldest and largest, but FAMU is the country's biggest historically black university.

Daytona 500
Since 1959, Daytona Beach has hosted the "Great American Race." With an average TV viewership of 20 million around the world, it's the most popular car race and one of the most-watched sporting events on TV. Cars fly around the 200 laps, covering 500 miles (hence the name) at speeds of up to 177 miles per hour!

Everglades
At the southern tip of Florida is a 1.5-million-acre preserve, the biggest subtropical wetland in North America. It's home to hundreds of animal species, many endangered, including the leatherback turtle, Florida panther, and West Indian manatee. And it's the only place on earth where crocodiles and alligators live together. Want to help protect this unique spot? Go to: www.evergladesfoundation.org.

Fort
European settlers built Florida's 100-plus forts starting in the 1500s. The oldest is Castillo de San Marcos, in St. Augustine. Constructed by the Spanish more than 340 years ago, it's shaped like a throwing star! The most unusual is Fort Jefferson, located seventy miles west of the Keys, atop one tiny coral island among many called the Dry Tortugas.

Gator
While Florida has a whopping 1.3 million alligators, there have been just twenty-three deadly attacks in the past sixty-eight years. More Floridians die from lightning strikes! The average female lays thirty-eight eggs, but only five of those gators will make it to adulthood. While the American alligator is Florida's state reptile, it is also an endangered species.

Hurricane
Hurricanes can be hundreds of miles across, with winds and rain spinning up to 200 miles per hour. They form over the ocean, but do real damage when they hit land. Hurricanes slam Florida more than any other state—114 times since 1851! Nearly twice as many as the next unluckiest state (Texas)! Strangely, hurricanes strike Florida more often in even years than odd (sixty-three vs fifty-two).

Facts about the

Indigenous People

Florida's indigenous people lived here more than 12,000 years before Europeans arrived. Explorers met dozens of groups, but by 1800 most were gone. Some died fighting the invaders, but most died from European diseases, which they had no immunity to. Today, 4,000 Seminole and Miccosukee people live on six reservations across the state.

Jacksonville

Jax, as locals call it, is a music town. It hosts one of the biggest, longest-running blues festivals in the country. *And* the second-biggest jazz festival. It was a movie town, too. During the 1910s, dozens of silent film studios opened in town. Monster movie classic *The Creature from the Black Lagoon* was filmed there.

Key West

This island city sits at the end of 800 Florida Keys that stretch over 180 miles! Four miles long and one mile wide, it's the southernmost point in the US. Spanish settlers called it "Cayo Hueso," meaning "Bone Island," for the Calusa Indian bones that littered the site. English speakers mispronounced it as "Key West."

Lake Okeechobee

Okeechobee, meaning "big water," is Florida's largest freshwater lake. It covers 730 square miles—about half the size of Rhode Island! It's super shallow—average depth is just nine feet! The Big O is a great place to fish for bass, crappie, and bluegill.

Manatee

A large aquatic mammal most closely related to the elephant, adults manatees are about ten feet long and weigh 800 to 1,200 pounds. They live in shallow, slow-moving waters and eat mostly plants. They are a protected species due to human threats, like boats and habitat destruction.

Nesting Turtle

Five types of sea turtle nest on Florida beaches—green, leatherback, loggerhead, Kemp's ridley, and hawksbill. They are air-breathing reptiles even though they spend 90 percent of their life in the ocean! On nights from March to October, females come ashore, dig pits, deposit 50 to 200 eggs, cover them with sand, and return to the sea.

Orange

Spanish explorers planted the first orange trees here in the mid-1500s. Florida makes more orange juice than anywhere else in the world except Brazil, squeezing 90 percent of the juice Americans drink. The citrus industry earns nine billion dollars a year! No wonder orange juice is the official state beverage.

Panther

These rare, solitary cats live in the forests and swamps of southern Florida, eating wild hogs, deer, raccoon, and armadillo. They can't roar, but instead communicate with whistles, chirps, hisses, and purrs. Although endangered due to habitat loss, the Florida panther population has been increasing in recent years, from only 20 panthers in 1970 to 160 in 2013.

Quinceañera

This coming-of-age celebration can be traced back to the Aztecs, when girls were given the responsibilities of womanhood. Today, traditions include a church ceremony, a father-daughter dance, and a big party for friends and family. Over four million Floridians have Hispanic ancestry (23 percent of the population).

great state of Florida

Rocket

Since 1947, the Kennedy Space Center has been the main US launch site for missiles, satellites, and manned space flights. Neil Armstrong, the first man on the moon, launched here, as did space shuttles from 1981 to 2011. Visitors to the complex can watch launches, tour the sights, and even meet real astronauts!

Sea Life

Stretching beside the Keys for 170 miles is the Florida Reef—North America's biggest coral reef! Forming over 10,000 years, today it shelters nearly 1,400 different kinds of plants and animals. Those waters are home to more sharks than any other place in the world including tiger, hammerhead, bull, lemon, reef, black tip, mako, dusky, and nurse sharks!

Theme Park

With more attractions than anywhere on earth, Orlando is the "Theme-Park Capital of the World." From Gatorland, the oldest, opened in 1949, to Walt Disney World Resort, the most popular theme park in the world with fifty-two million visitors a year! There's also LEGOLAND, Wizarding World of Harry Potter (Universal Studios), SeaWorld, Busch Gardens, and more.

Underwater Research Lab

The Aquarius Reef Base is an undersea laboratory operated by Florida International University. It's located in the ocean sixty-two feet below the surface, next to a deep coral reef. Scientists and students use the lab for research, education, training, and technology development. Now that's a cool school!

Vacation

With a record-setting ninety-seven million visitors in 2014, Florida is the No. 1 travel destination in the world! Vacationers come for the theme parks, beaches, and sunshine. Florida's weather is pretty great—average temperatures are between 61°F in the winter and 82°F in the summer.

Weeki Wachee Springs

One of Florida's oldest attractions, Weeki Wachee Springs is so deep, the bottom has never been found! More than 100 million gallons of water bubble up daily from underground caverns. In 1947 a dive instructor built an underground theater and taught girls how to perform while breathing from hidden air hoses. The park's mermaids drink soda, eat bananas, and do aquatic ballet, all underwater.

eXtreme Sports

Surrounded by ocean, Florida is an awesome place to try extreme water sports. You can surf, scuba dive, kiteboard, jet ski . . . the sky's the limit! Flyboarding is the newest fad. You stand on a board as water shoots out from jets underneath, pushing you high into the air. Blast off!

Yummy

A Key West cook named "Aunt Sally" first made Key lime pie in the early 1900s. Created from ingredients common to the islands and ships that sailed to them at that time: Key limes (which grow there), egg yolks, and sweetened condensed milk. The ingredients needed no refrigeration and the tart and tangy pie needed no cooking.

Zebra Longwing

This tropical butterfly eats the leaves of passionflowers, which are toxic and make the insect poisonous. Its bold stripes warn predators: don't eat me! It also wiggles its body to make a creaking noise when bothered. At night, large groups of zebra longwings roost together in trees, returning to the same spot each night. Sweet dreams, butterfly!

Thank you to everyone at Boys & Girls Clubs of Central Florida for encouraging your kids to write and enter this contest. Thank you to the dedicated staff, and Anwar Hunte at the Club's Cocoa branch, who guided the youth through this process. And most of all, thanks to the kids who wrote such fantastic poetry for this book. Way to go!

Boys & Girls Clubs of Central Florida focuses on providing disadvantaged youth with enriching programs that lead to academic success, healthy lifestyles and positive character and citizenship. Club youth benefit from a safe, positive environment, supportive relationships with caring adults and mentors, unique educational and career opportunities, and a variety of fun programs that help build an optimistic foundation for the future. To learn more about the Boys & Girls Clubs of Central Florida, visit our website at

The Authors of *F is for Florida*

Belen Hernandez	Ariauna Strickland	Julionna Foster
Tameya Moore	Frank Scott	Julius Harris
Tarameka Moore	Ci'Miya Davis	Treyonna Davis
Daija Davis	Ashton Davis	Brooklyn Jones
Bonicia Bartlette	Riley McClain	

Text © 2017 by WestWinds Press®

The following photographers hold copyright to their images as indicated: iStock.com/Pgiam, **A**; iStock.com/jhorrocks, **B**; iStock.com/Aneese, **C**; iStock.com/avid_creative, **D**; iStock.com/Yobro10, **E**; iStock.com/JayAndersons, **F**; iStock.com/clark42, **G**; iStock.com/ChiehCheng, **H**; iStock.com/Juanmonino, **I**; iStock.com/SeanPavonePhoto, **J**; iStock.com/no-limit-pictures, **K, front cover (bottom)**; iStock.com/irabassi, **L**; iStock.com/NaluPhoto, **M**; iStock.com/Karliux_, **N**; iStock.com/MoJoStudio, **O, front cover (top)**; iStock.com/fotoguy22, **P**; iStock.com/GemaBlanton, **Q**; iStock.com/CelsoDiniz, **R**; iStock.com/AndrewJalbert, **S**; iStcok.com/cristianl, **T**; Florida International University Aquarius Reef Base, **U**; iStock.com/tap10, **V**; Andrew Brusso, **W**; iStock.com/Eric betoon, **X**; iStock.com/Warren_Price, **Y**; iStock.com/patty_c , **Z, back cover.**

All rights reserved. No part of this book may be reproduced or transmitted in any form or by any means, electronic or mechanical, including photocopying, recording, or by any information storage and retrieval system, without written permission of the publisher.

Library of Congress Cataloguing-in-Publication Data
Title: F is for Florida / written by kids for kids.
Description: Portland, Oregon : WestWinds Press, 2017. |
  Audience: K to grade 3.
Identifiers: LCCN 2017005209
  ISBN 9781513141862 (paperback)
  ISBN 9781513260495 (hardcover)
  ISBN 9781513260501 (electronic)
Subjects: LCSH: Florida—Juvenile literature. | English
  language—Alphabet—Juvenile literature.
Classification: LCC F311.3 .F33 2017 | DDC 975.9—dc23
LC record available at https://lccn.loc.gov/2017005209

WestWinds Press®
An imprint of of Turner Publishing Company
4507 Charlotte Avenue, Suite 100
Nashville, TN 37209
(615) 255-2665
www.turnerbookstore.com

Editor: Michelle McCann
Designer: Vicki Knapton

Part of the See-My-State Series, Written by Kids for Kids!

Printed in the USA
CPSIA information can be obtained
at www.ICGtesting.com
JSHW072027140824
68134JS00042B/3816